Pierre Fierre Loses a Dare!

by JSB Morse

Copyright © 2023 by JSB Morse. All Rights Reserved. Printed in the United States of America. Holy Scripture from Proverbs 16:18 and Luke 14:11.

This book was produced by Libertas Kids, an imprint of Code Publishing, Austin, TX. LibertasKids.com
ISBN 978-1-60020-107-3 Ebook: 978-1-60020-108-0

Deep in the bayou where the swamp meets the land,
King Pierre Fierre ruled with an iron hand.
For he was the biggest, the strongest, and best,
His roars echoed loudly when he beat on his chest.

Every day he made all his subjects sing a hymn,
And begrudgingly they all lifted their voices for him.

Hail King Pierre Fierre, with power and pomp,
The most handsomest beast who ever lived in the swamp.
With bumps and ridges on your tail so grand,
You make us so proud to live in your land.

With a noble snout and a stately jaw,
And regal talons that leave us in awe.
Oh King Pierre Fierre, so grand and so strong,
We're so honored to slave for you all day long.

He'd dance and he'd strut, oh, so full of pride,
As he marched by his subjects with an arrogant stride.

But one little creature, a turtle named Beau,
Decided he'd had enough of the show.
So, he turned his back on the song and dance,
And that startled the others right out of their trance.

Pierre saw this slight and he let out a shout.
"How dare you not worship your master, you lout!?"
Beau said, "Sorry I won't worship or sing,
For I only bow to the one and true King."
"Hey, I am the ruler of this here swamp, Beau.
Sing for me T, or I'll make you into gumbo!"

Beau pondered his choices, a weight on his chest,
Should he sing with the others or put courage to test?
But the gator was too big and he had no chance,
So he put a foot forward and started to dance.

Pierre laughed. "That's better kid. That's how it should be. All of my subjects must always praise me!"

That night under the moon's silvery gleam,
Beau gathered the animals to hatch up a scheme.
He spoke with conviction in the humid night air,
"Let's unite together and overthrow Pierre!"

But the animals all scoffed, "There's just no way, Beau.
Pierre's just too strong, from his snout to his toe."
Beau shook his head, "There must be a way,"
And then, Evangeline, the owl, had her say.

"Pierre is mighty, but he's prouder than all,
And pride, as they say, goes before the fall.
Beau's right there's a way. I have seen it from the air.
With help from above we can get rid of Pierre!"

So the animals worked together to come up with a plan,
To overthrow the despot and bring peace to the land.

The next morning everyone lined up ready to sing,
Except for little Beau, defying the king.

Pierre grinned wide at the treacherous sight.
"So, I guess it's turtle soup for breakfast, all right!"
Beau said, "Wait a minute there, Tyrannosaur!
Before you eat me, may I please have the floor?"

"You think you're so marvelous and big and smart,
But you have no compassion, no guts, and no heart!"
"I challenge you to a race," Beau declared with some flair,
"To that hill with the sign over there if you dare."

"No thanks," said Pierre, "I'll just eat you right here."
"What's the matter?" asked Beau. "Do I smell fear?"
Pierre chuckled with a quick and sly grin,
"All right, I'll race you, but don't think you'll win!
This isn't some fable and I ain't no hare,
I'm the fastest and smartest. I'm Pierre Fierre!"

The lightning bugs signaled the start of the race,
And Pierre tore off leaving Beau in his wake.
They raced to the sign, Pierre won, it was clear,
And everyone was quiet so he made them all cheer.

As they cheered for their king, in the midst of their hymn,
The creatures stopped singing and just stared at him.
"What's the matter, Cher?" Pierre asked with a frown,
When hunters with a snare and a net took him down.

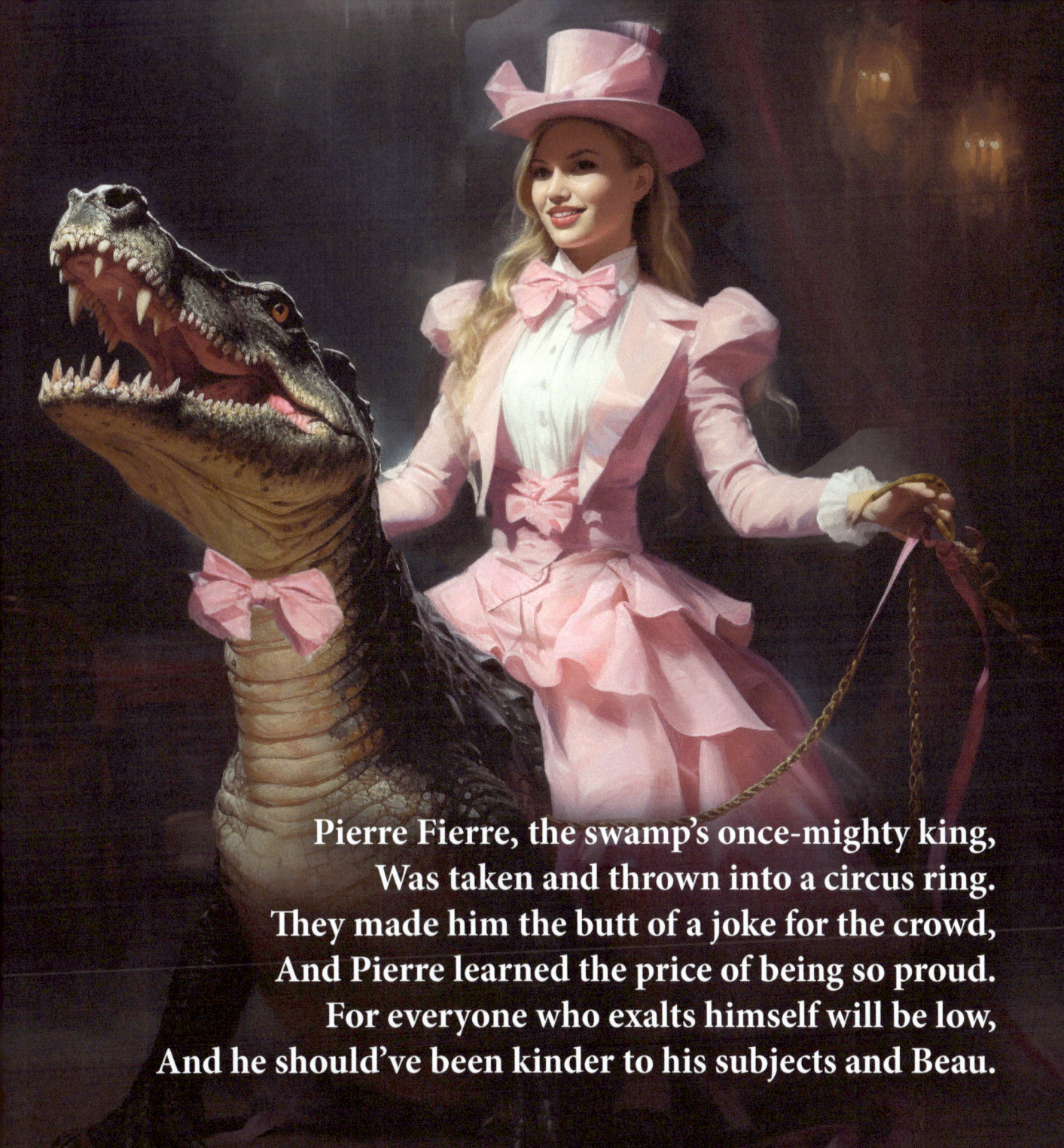

And Beau, the turtle, so meek and so small,
Had proven that pride causes the mighty to fall.

All the animals said, "For Beau, we'll now sing!"
But Beau said, "No, for God is the King."

THE END.

For more great stories, visit LibertasKids.com!